Potatoes In The Cellar
And Other Tales

David J Morris

Dedicated to all my friends
when we were young:
Monty, Freddy, Alan, Catherine, Pat, Anthea and others far
too many to mention – although honestly, I can't for the life
of me remember who they were?

Introduction

Before 1974, Morley was in The West Riding Of Yorkshire –
and to many, including myself, still is. It became a Municipal
Borough in 1889 and under the Local Government Act 1972,
was incorporated into the City of Leeds Metropolitan District,
and in 1974, West Yorkshire was formed as a
new metropolitan county.

Many Yorkshire folk drop their aitches (but strangely not all the
time), lose the letter 'g' in words ending 'ing' and use an
abbreviated form of the words 'into' and 'the'.
For example: In the phrase,
"I was going into the house," would be: "I was goin' in' t'ouse." –
but there again, often using 'were' instead of 'was'. And other
vagaries in 'Yorkspeak' is the omission of 'f' in 'of', and
sometimes even saying 'on' for 'of'.
Also there is the employment of 'yer' for the words 'you' and
'your', and 'yer're' for 'you're'.
Another weird thing is the use of 'sen' for 'self' as in 'hersen' and
mesen (myself), but never 'himsen' when 'hissen' is used instead.
On occasions, a hard 'i' (as in die), is softened to produce 'dee',
and the word 'out' is pronounced as 'aht' –
and similarly, 'about' as 'abaht'.

Contents
***

Part One
(Page 9 with image)

Part Two

(Page 45 with image)

Part Three

(Page 69 with image)

Part One
The Early Years

The Nipper

One particular day, my mother was taking me in my push-chair to my aunts' house when she stopped at a fish shop for – yes, some fish. And you may remember that they usually had an open, sloping shelf on the street, displaying various cooked shellfish. Here the fishmonger was setting out new items for the day's sale, and in seeing us, said to Mam, "Nay, lass. That babby o' thine is big enough to ger aht an' push thee!" And with that, he laughed and went back in his shop.

Leaving me outside (that would be unheard of these days), Mam followed him in to purchase what she wanted, and then we went on our way to my aunts.

When we got there, Mam deposited her shopping; and while one of my aunts put the items away, my mother took the covers off the pram to take me out, only to find me cuddling a crab.

She did consider returning the thing to the shop, but couldn't bear to have to admit that her son, barely out of nappies, was a thief.

So they had it for tea with a bit of salad.

Danger On Line

At one time, there were two railway stations in Morley: Morley Top and Morley Low. My early life was spent on Hunger Hill, which was close to Morley Top.

For as long as I can remember, I have always been fascinated by trains – especially those using coal to produce steam. Later in my life when we used Morley Low to go on club trips from Ackroyd Street Working Men's Club, I always recall my mother telling me not to look out of the window in case I got sparks in my eyes – in fact, I did once. Anyhow, I digress, so let me get back to my tale.

As a young lad of five or six, I wanted to explore everything that life had to offer, and I did – especially the temptation of trains. One day, I went up to Morley Top and, from what I remember, the platform was just to the right of the little booking office and easily accessible. Being little at the time, no one saw me sneak onto the platform and wait for a train to turn up. There wasn't anybody else around, and, unhindered, I patiently waited until I was rewarded when a train arrived. I think it must have been a goods train or one not really going anywhere, since after the driver asked me if I'd like a ride, I eagerly accepted his invite and we went for a short journey before returning to the station.

I was so excited that I ran home and innocently told my mam of my adventure, but was shocked at her reaction: she shook me repeatedly and vehemently scolded me. I must have cried because I didn't realise what I had done wrong, but of course now I do. It was a "don't accept sweets from strangers" moment, and I guess – even in those days – I was lucky not to have been abused or suffered something much worse! Yes, my mother's admonishment truly made me think about the dangers in this most disturbing world.

The New Rug

I remember Mam making 'list' rugs – or rag rugs as they were often called – and many of you will be familiar with them I'm sure.

You'd stretch a piece of hessian over a frame on trestles and pull it taught by sticking pegs into the holes in the frame, then prod the rags through with a wooden 'skewer'.

One winter, my mother decided to make a new one for in front of the hearth. It was a pride and joy to us, and Mam wanted to keep it in pristine condition. So, when it was bath time for me, she'd get the tin bath from the cellar head (never was it stuck on a hook on the outside wall, and it wasn't the size of a horse trough), but she wouldn't put it on the new rug in front of the fire – even on this winter's day – so she decided to plonk it in the large stoneware sink. You may be wondering why she didn't just take the rug up and put it directly on the flagstones, well so do I now considering that above the sink was a shelf displaying certain items of crockery. But what Mam decided, had to be.

She'd then boil water on the fire or on the one gas ring we had – or to make sure there was enough hot water for me, one pan on the ring and another on the open fire. Then I was deposited in the bath – in the sink – and soaped up.

Being winter, the water soon got cold before my bath was finished, so she heated more water on the gas; but because the pan was full and she wanted to add some cold water so that it wouldn't be too hot for me, she poured some down the sink. Of course, by the law of conduction, the hot water permeated the tin bath and I shot up and banged my head on the shelf, causing the crockery to come crashing down onto the stone-flagged floor. And while I stood there holding my head and rubbing my backside, all my mother could say was: "Nay, David. Just look what you've done to me best pots!"

How I suffered at times.

The Miracle

There came a time after my father died, when Mam decided it was time for us to have a bit of a treat instead of constantly grieving; so, even though it was a bit of a struggle, she booked for the two of us to spend a few days over Christmas in Blackpool.

She arranged with a neighbour – the kindly Mrs Buckley who lived next door to us – to see to my elderly, paternal grandmother until we returned. My grandma was a bit of a difficult person, but Mrs Buckley said that if the woman caused any problems, she'd empty the piss-pot over her. And believe me, she would have done.

Anyhow, when I woke up on Christmas morning in the lodging-house, Santa hadn't been. I can't say I was terribly disappointed because I knew my mother would have had to scrape together every penny she possessed for the trip – and besides, I was ready for my breakfast.

Downstairs, a lot of the other kids were in tears because they also hadn't received any presents, but me – well, I just tucked into my egg, bacon, and fried bread without really caring. Then a miracle occurred.

Down the road outside the B&B, came the jingling of donkey bells as the animals were on their way to the sands – even though it was winter. And then they stopped outside the window, whence we all looked out. They were actually pulling Santa Claus. We watched him get off his 'sleigh' and come inside where he gave us each our own special gift.

It was a Christmas I will never forget.

Thanks Mam. xx

The Firebrand

As an introduction to my aunt Maria – pronounced with a hard 'i' as in 'fire': the word itself being most appropriate for this remarkable woman.

After her mother died in 1933, Maria was thirty-seven and unmarried. At the time, my own mother was nineteen and my Aunt Emma even younger. They were Maria's half-sisters – born to her mother after her second marriage. Then after their mother died, and having no surviving father, Maria took on a maternal responsibility for her younger sisters. The three females were rehoused from Banks Buildings on Wide Lane to Troy Road, and when Emma was married, she and her husband lived in the same house. My mam married in 1944 and moved out to a place on Hunger Hill with my dad and his own mother.

Aunt Maria was a good Catholic woman who didn't like people swearing. I remember once saying that something was 'rotten' and she was outraged, but didn't hold back with the words 'bloody' or 'bugger' – or even worse. She was a total, but adorable, enigma.

And she was mischievous: often starting an argument between my mother and cousin only to sit back and giggle as they carried on the row. She was second only to my mam on the love scale.

The Snip

When I was very young, I hated going to the barber's since I was always getting hair clippings in my eyes or on my face; and the barber used to get annoyed at me constantly either using my hand to brush them away, or blowing them off the best I could.

One day, my mother took me to a barber shop on Wesley Street and gave him instructions on how she wanted it cutting, then told me that when it was done to go straight to my aunt Maria's.

"Aaw, don't leave me Mam," I pleaded. "It's 'orrible 'ere."

Grabbing my arm now, she growled, "Get in that bloody chair afore I leather yer. There'll be no tea for yer today if yer don't." So I complied, whereby Mam paid the barber and left to go to work at Peel Street Mill.

As soon as the barber put the white 'sheet' over me and began snipping, the hairs were on my face again and I decided that I was taking no more punishment. So, I sprang from the chair – still with the sheet around me – and ran from the shop, chasing after my mam like a demented moth before she got to work. I refused to go back, so she had to stuff the sheet in her bag and take me to the mill with her with half-cut hair.

As I grew, I became less stroppy about having a haircut and used to go to the Town Hall Barbers. Knowing that I was going on a certain day, my cousin – who was always playing pranks on me – asked me to get him a cigar for his dad, which apparently the barber sold, and told me the brand he wanted. So after my hair was done, I said to the barber, "Oh, and could I 'ave a Rubber Johnny for me cousin?"

I never went back to that barber's either.

Tripe

Since my mother worked when I was young, I spent a great deal of time at my aunts' house: my aunt Emma and, of course, the ever faithful, ever present, Maria.

My aunt Em had to go in hospital once, so Aunt Maria asked me to go to the butcher in Morley Market for some tripe (horrible stuff) for my uncle's tea. Now, my mother had always brought me up to speak properly – no dropping of aitches and saying thee, or 'tha knors' for 'you know' – and to always be polite (although, I did slip up at times). Anyhow, my aunt wrote down what was needed and sent me on my way. But, unbeknown to me, one of the items was a colloquialism she used.

I got to the butcher's and, not wanting to appear like a baby, I didn't pass the note over but – in my most succinct and well-mannered voice – read. "I would like half a pound of honeycomb," says I.

"Reight, lad," said the butcher. "And owt else?"

I referred to my note, answering, "Yes. And please could I have six or seven inches of cobbler's knob."

And from that day to this, I have never found out – or wanted to know – what sort of strange product that is.

Feast Week

It was always Blackpool for us on Morley's annual holiday when all the woollen mills shut down. My mam – like many others – got her Co-op divi and it paid for the holiday.

As I mentioned before, they were exciting times for me: having breakfast in the boarding-house and hearing the jingling of the bells on the donkeys going passed the window on their way to the sands – so much so that I pestered the life out of Mam to buy me a Muffin the Mule puppet, which, after going in nearly every shop in the town, we eventually found.

One year, I remember a plague of flies invading the beach, and there were so many of them, they covered the white ice-cream vans and turned them black. Another year my cousin and her daughter came with us and they wanted to visit the Tower Zoo – so we all went.

It wasn't to my own and my mam's taste, and proved to be ill-starred for my cousin when, standing close to the cage and pulling faces at one of the lions (likely a lioness), it turned about, pressed its backside against the bars and – with the force of a fireman's hose – urinated all over her.

Yes, they were happy days.

Moving

After my father died and my ailing grandma – his mother – was settled into an old-folks home, we moved.

Being young at the time, I can only imagine that the house was required for a family larger than just Mam and I. And it happened that we got a small house on Troy Road near to my aunts. I loved Troy Road – especially in winter when snow was on the ground.

My mam had an enamelled tray with curved edges, which she used next to the sink on top of the wooden draining-board to contain the drips off wet washing-up and prevent them from staining the bare, unprotected wood.

Our house was number 65, and was just at a point where Troy Road becomes steep as it runs down to Albert Road; so, on snow-hardened days, I'd sit on the tray and go hell for leather all the way down. And I never stopped at the bottom, but would shoot across Albert Road without looking for traffic and down the dirt track (iced over of course) known as Bilberry Bank, and slide on my tray sledge all the way down to Station Road. The only thing I didn't like was walking all the way back carrying a blue enamelled tray.

Nevertheless, temptation got the better of me and I was off again....

The Card-Sharp

Every year on Christmas Day, the family went to my cousin's house for dinner. Then on Boxing Day, she and her daughter would come to my aunt Maria's for stand-pie and pickles and other nibbles.

After the nibbling was over, we young ones would plonk ourselves on the hearth-rug and occupy ourselves in some game or other while the adults gathered around the table and played Newmarket.

There are a number of variations of this card-game and I won't delve into the details of each, but just say it's a 'follow-on' game; and in my family's version, Aces were low. Four Queens are taken from a second pack – or roughly drawn on pieces of paper if you haven't a spare. They are placed on the table with a space between them for the 'kitty', and a dummy hand is dealt for anyone who may receive a poor set of cards and wants to swap – but they had to pay a previously agreed price into the kitty. The dealer gets first choice of a swap, and if he or she doesn't need it, then the player to their left has the choice – and so on.

The dealer begins by playing their lowest card (of any suit of their choice) and others follow on. If no one can play a card, the player who puts down the last one, starts another round with a new low card. And so it progresses until anyone with a Queen claims the money on that card, and the player who gets rid of all their cards first, receives the kitty.

There came a point when the Queen of Hearts had amassed a substantial amount of cash, and having watchful eyes, I spotted my cousin surreptitiously remove the said Queen from the pack when it was her deal and place it on her knee – hoping that the Jack would eventually come out and she could use the stolen card to claim the cash.

It was then I decided to stop her cheating ways, so I nonchalantly took a little meander and noticed that Mam, who was sitting to my cousin's right, held the Jack in her own hand. So, I determined to turn the tables on my cousin.

I returned to messing about on the rug as the game began, and at a convenient point, gently removed the Queen from my cousin's knee, tapped my mother's leg, and passed over the card. And then I waited....

The Nine of Hearts was played, then the Ten, and then my mother could play both Jack and Queen and claim the amount as my cousin looked about her in bewilderment. And to rub salt in the wound, my mother also went on to claim the kitty!

Nobody got the better of other folk – especially his mam – when David was around.

The Secret

My aunt Mary lived on Middleton Road and her husband was a chimney-sweep; and I always remember that they still had an Anderson shelter in the back garden left over from the war. Presumably having done some washing, she was there in the garden when we arrived on a visit, and Mam said quietly, "She's hanging out those drawers of hers again, so there goes another bloody hour of daylight."

Every year on my birthday, my mam and I were invited to tea when Aunt Mary used to give me a present. She must have run out of ideas for gifts as I grew older, and decided cash would be more appropriate. But Aunt Mary didn't believe in banks, and kept her cash in some secret place only known to herself.

On this special day, we had finished tea and then she disappeared, saying, "Now both of yer close yer eyes, and I'll go and get yer present, our David." While she was away, my mam said, "An' this time you're saving the money. I'm not 'avin' you spendin' it on spice (sweets)."

But my aunt was gone a heck of a long time. "Oh, I can't sit here any longer wi' me bloody eyes shut," said Mam. "C'mon, let's go and see where the hell she is."

So we stood and went on a search of the whole house – including the shelter – until we finally found her in the bedroom with ten bob and pound notes scattered around her feet while she was trapped under the mattress.

We heaved the mattress off her, and led her back to the front room where Mam made her a cup of sweet tea. And when Aunt Mary had recovered sufficiently, I was given my present and eventually we left.

Once outside, my mother's reaction was: "I didn't think chimney-sweeps made so much? Mind you, she'll have to find a new place to keep her brass, now. And I dread to think where that might be?"

The Itch

One day I was ill and off school. And since my mother was working, I was staying at my aunts' house.

My cousin, who was six years older than myself, was in senior school whilst I was still in the juniors; and at one point his parents were told to buy him a support for PT – otherwise known as a jock-strap.

I was with my aunt Maria when Aunt Emma returned after taking my cousin to see the doctor after he developed some sort of 'condition'.

"Well, what was it, lass?" asked Aunt Maria of her sister.

"Eeh, Maria," said my aunt Em, "the doctor says it's summat called jock-itch."

"Aye, it's surprising what kids pick up at school off their mates – like nits."

"Any'ow," says my aunt Emma, "he's gone back to school now and is going to ask one of his friends to come for tea."

"Nay, our David's badly, Em," said Aunt Maria; "so I hope it's not Jock 'at's comin'. Apart from 'em talkin' so bloody funny, I couldn't abide a Scotch lad in t"ouse scrattin' hissen an' passin' summat on."

Our Ver

Now I must redress the balance and talk about my aunt Veronica.

She was the 'lady' of the family: house-proud, well-spoken, and compared to her other sisters, relatively well-off. And whenever my mam took me for a visit – which wasn't that often – I enjoyed the experience because we always had cream cakes for tea.

One day in a school holiday while my mother went to work, I was left in my aunt Maria's charge. "Now," my mother said, "what are you two getting up to today?"

"Well," said Aunt Maria. "I thought we'd go and see our Ver." (Veronica was always know as that shortened version of her name.)

At first, Mam was a little taken aback at the suggestion, but said, "Well make sure our David (I was mentioned as if I wasn't in the room) weshes (washes) behind 'is lugs."

"I did 'em this mornin', Mam," says I. "Well do 'em again," said my mother and left for work. When she was out of earshot, Aunt Maria said, "Oh, don't bother, lad, They'll be clean enough." So we got ready and set off.

Once at Aunt Veronica's house, we settled down for afternoon tea, whence she said, "What do you think of my curtains, Hannah?"

Now you see, Aunt Veronica always referred to her sister by her true first name, and this was an intolerable irritant to Aunt Maria, who got up and went to the window where she felt the material. "I think they're like our David's lugs," says she.

"What do you mean?" said Veronica as puzzled as I was.

Returning to the table, Aunt Maria remarked in her customary candid way, "They could do wi' a wesh."

Why did I always have to be involved!?

Toilet Humour

To begin with, most of you will recall having to use an outside toilet which was often shared with a neighbour (or more than just one), and sometimes they were situated quite a distance from the house. And this little story involves one.

My cousin was spoiled rotten: he would ask his parents for something and usually get it. He once acquired a kit for making crystal sets, which were popular with kids at the time, and he told me he'd make me one. But my mother – for some reason only known to herself – said that she didn't want me having such a contraption, and if I brought it into the house she'd throw it out.

Yet my cousin and I had different plans; and when he'd completed it, we sneaked it out of my aunts' house where my mother and they were gossiping away.

You'll likely remember in those days we rarely locked our doors, so the two of us were able to get in to my place and set it up in the bedroom. My cousin placed it on the window-sill and leaned out to fix the aerial on a convenient hook on the outside wall.

It was then I happened to look up the street and catch sight of my mam leaving my aunts' house to come home. We both bolted outside before she saw us and fled in different directions, myself taking a route at the side of the block.

Now this is where the lavatory comes into the tale. Ours, and the neighbour's, was situated at the bottom of a steep slope at the side of our houses, and I was running so fast I realised I wouldn't be able to stop and would probably crash into the toilet door and bash my head in. But lo and behold the door was slightly open and I went straight inside – landing comfortably in the lap of our neighbour who was sitting there.

I won't tell you what he yelled at me, but it did involve the task at hand. And oddly enough, he never spoke to me and Mam again.

Aunt Emma

Aunt Em was the baby of the many sisters in the family in more senses than one: she was small and thin and gentle; and – unlike my mother and Aunt Maria – was never a gossip. And I loved her for her innocence.

She was married in 1939 and gave birth to my cousin a year later – and she doted on her son, who was spoiled beyond the average for any boy. After I was born six years later and began to grow up beyond my years, my cousin and I fought like cat and dog. I don't know whether it was because I was jealous of him getting everything he asked for from his parents whilst, by this time, my father had died and Mam and I had little to spend on fripperies; or if he disliked me for being 'more intelligent' for a lad six years his junior.

I was about twelve when Aunt Em was diagnosed with cancer and had an operation on her neck. My aunt Maria said it would do no good because – and I quote her own words: "When they cut yer, the air gets in and yer're a goner." Now whether or not this was a medical fact in those days, I know not; but Aunt Maria's supposition proved to be true when Aunt Em died shortly afterwards. She was only in her early forties.

It soon came to light after the heart-breaking event, that my uncle (Aunt Em's husband) had been 'playing away' during her short illness and he soon remarried and moved out, leaving his son in the care of the elderly Maria. I guess that's why Mam and I spent so much time at the house on Troy Road – to help out in the best way we could.

After that, my cousin was devastated at the loss of both parents and sank into an abject depression. It was then we grew closer to each other; and, despite having been sworn enemies on certain previous occasions, we became like loving brothers.

And – together with so many others – I miss him now.

Going Camping

They say the simple pleasures are the best.

When Mam and I had lived on Newlands Drive for a few years after being rehoused, she gave up work and lived – well, existed – on a widow's pension. In order to supplement this, she looked after my cousin's young daughter in school holidays while my cousin went to work.

Every weekday, I would get the 55 Bruntcliffe bus on Wide Lane to the Hembrigg pub on High Street, collect the youngster from where she lived in Hembrigg Terrace, and then we were just in time to get the same bus back home.

On certain days, my mother would take some of our – and Aunt Maria's – washing to a launderette opposite the Fountain Inn on Queen Street. Then when it was done (even watching it go round in the machine was a pleasure – but not likely for Mam), the three of us would toddle off to Troy Road, and while Mam helped out with a bit of cleaning in my aunt's house, myself and my cousin once removed, played out. One lovely sunny day, I told my mam that we were going camping. "Well don't go far," she said. "And don't be longer than half an hour....Have yer got yer watch on?" I told her I had and set about the preparations.

In order to construct a tent, I borrowed my aunt's wooden clothes-horse, a rag rug from the kitchen and an old blanket to drape over the opened-out horse. And in the area where the makeshift tent was constructed, we'd play away merrily until I looked at my watch and decided that it was time for us to go home for dinner. So we exited the tent and walked the few yards up the garden path and into the house.

Well after all, Mam *had* told me not to go far.

The Finger

As a very small child, I was interested in everything – especially words.

I was lying on the floor one day flipping through a dictionary – of all things – and came across a word whose pronunciation and definition made no sense to me at my age. So, I asked my mam: "Mam. What is a pennis?"

Curiously, she took the book off me to see what I was referring to, and when she realised what I'd been looking at, she said sternly, "Come and get yer dinner!"

So my education – or lack of it – always seemed to happen at mealtimes. My mother and my aunt used some weird expressions when talking about things, and this is in a similar vein.

One day, I was dispatched to the scullery to keep an eye on dinner and heard them talking about a neighbour being found dead in the outside lav playing with his 'middle finger'. I was totally confused since I'd never heard of somebody dying just by doing that, so I went and asked what they meant. My mother glared at me for listening in and, pointing a finger, said, "Get back in that kitchen and see to those sausages."

She'd done it to me again!

Part Two
The Formative Years

Potatoes In The Cellar

After my aunt Emma died, my aunt Maria was convinced that her younger sister's spirit was visiting her during the night. Even at my youthful age, I was sceptical about the existence of 'ghosts' and believed it to be my aunt's imagination.

My mother asked me to get a sack of potatoes from the cellar head so she could start making something for tea, so I obliged. As I lifted the sack, I suddenly heard footsteps coming up at me from the depths of the black-dark cellar, and I dropped the sack causing the potatoes to cascade down into darkness as I bolted back to the front room. "Where's me mam?" I asked my aunt in a panic.

"She's just gone upstairs," she replied. "What the 'ell's up?"

"There's summat comin' up t'cellar steps!"

"What sort o' bloody summat?" my aunt asked. Then, as my mother began to descend from above, it dawned on me that since the creaky bedroom stairs ran directly above those of the cellar, it was my mother's steps which I'd heard. I felt like a total imbecile.

For a long time afterwards, I was reluctant to go anywhere near that gloomy place – although I was made to go and gather up the potatoes. But not without making sure the light was firmly on.

Lest We Forget

My aunt Maria always wore her poppy with pride. So much so that when a parade for Remembrance Day took place in Roundhay Park in Leeds one year, she decided to take part. She bought a 'kind of' black, cloche hat from a shop in Morley, and when she asked my mother what she thought of it, my mother's reply was lukewarm to say the least.

"Well, I've gone and bought the bugger, nar," said my aunt, "so it'll bloody well 'ave to do." Then on the day of the parade, Aunt Maria took the bus to the park – and Mam and I joined her there later.

We stood on a slope around the edge of the large arena to watch her march alongside the veterans of both world wars. I asked my mother how on earth we were going to catch a glimpse of her in all the people taking part. And, referring to my aunt's hat, she said, "Just look art for someb'dy wi' a soddin' German 'elmet on."

So I did. And I spotted her without any trouble.

The Brisling

The matriarchal Aunt Maria, had a penchant – unintentionally – for coming out with a number of malapropisms and spoonerisms.

In living up to Mrs Malaprop in Sheridan's play 'The Rivals', she excelled; so here are just a few of those. When talking about a neighbour whose son had 'gone a bit funny' she said, "She ought to take him to see a piechiatrist." On another occasion, she was talking about seeing a ghost one night. "But our Tony," she says to my mam, "told me it were nowt but a pigment of me imagination." And then there was the one about a neighbour's new baby boy when she said to Mam, "'Er next door's 'ad to 'ave the poor little bugger circumscribed." Another was told to me directly when my aunt was discussing a man she knew who was terrified of heights: "He can't go up a ladder 'cos o' sufferin' wi' verdigris."

And a few of the latter I have never forgotten, one such being when we suffered an sudden downpour and the insurance man was due at my aunt's house. When he arrived, she raced to the door, saying, "Come in quick, lad; yer're wettin' get." On another occasion, what she said to my mother when talking about my cousin was truly special: "Well, I'll tell yer this, Sally," she stated. "He's nowt but a boiled sprat."

How I loved my aunt Maria!

Thimble?

My aunt's neighbour, Emma, worked as a cleaner at the Leeds Skyrack And Morley Bank on the corner of Queen Street and Little Lane.

She was an intelligent and passionate church-goer, and attended the Methodist Church on Albert Road; and even when it moved to the Newlands Estate, she still walked there to attend a service. But Emma was somewhat deaf, and I remember a school project where I had to write an essay about the cross (in Christianity) as a symbol, so I decided that Emma would be the ideal person to help me.

I was staying at my aunt Maria's one evening, when Emma turned up – as she did every night with her supper and a mug of tea, to watch my aunt's TV since she didn't have one.

I thought this to be the best opportunity to pick her brain: "Emma!" I said – at a pitch I thought would be just loud enough so that she didn't have to adjust her hearing aid and cause it to whistle. "What do think of the cross as a symbol?" She leaned forward at me, saying, "What? Slots in a thimble?"

Well, my aunt Maria – a good Catholic woman – was flabbergasted, and shouted at Emma: "Slots in a thimble? Slots be buggered!"

Alas, I had to do my complicated essay without any help whatsoever.

The Drift

Aunt Maria loved fresh air and always kept the sash-window of her bedroom wide open.

One day when Mam and I visited her early in the morning after an unexpected snowstorm the previous night, my mother was surprised not to see her up. My cousin must have lit the fire before he went to work because it was blazing away nicely in the grate, and, thinking that my aunt may have died overnight, my mother asked me to accompany her upstairs to see if she had indeed kicked the bucket. (I was always co-opted into doing something that may have been a chilling experience – and it was.)

Aunt Maria was frozen under a blanket of snow with just her face sticking out of the drift – asleep! With my hands, I had to shovel the snow off her while my mother shook her into consciousness.

All my aunt could say after being dug out, was: "Oh, is it mornin' already, Sally…? Eeh, lass; it's bloody cold in 'ere."

And we had to help her downstairs to thaw out.

Gone To The Dogs

It's true now, as it was when I was young, that dogs do the funniest things. My first ever dog, Peggy, was a black Labrador...ish, and we (well, my mam really) bought her when we were rehoused from Troy Road to Newlands Drive.

She was a beautiful and faithful dog, but had one peculiar habit: she used to find the biggest stone she could (often a discarded half-brick) and joyfully carry it in her mouth for ages. On visits to my aunt's, as soon as we turned off Albert Road to go up Troy, she was allowed off the lead. Here, she would search out the predictable brick in the ruins of our old home, and cart it to my aunt's house where she duly dropped it on her feet. We always knew she was indoors (the door was always open) when my aunt could be heard screaming expletives.

Next door to us on the Newlands Estate, was a family who left their own dog (a 'sort of' fox terrier) outside day in and day out and in all weathers, and when we mentioned it to my aunt, she was horrified and asked my mam to see if the people would let her have him. They agreed, and Maria got the dog; but, he kept running back home and sitting at the door of his old house.

Nonetheless, with our frequent persistence, he soon realised where his bread was buttered and finally settled on Troy Road, positioning himself at the back of my aunt on her chair beside the hearth.

Now, Aunt Maria had the painful prospect of being assaulted not only by a Labrador with half a brick, but a fox terrier stretching his legs out and almost shoving her into the fire.

Poor Maud

This little tale concerns a friend of my mother called Maud. She lived in a block of three houses on Wide Lane, and for some reason she was always known as 'Poor Maud'.

The situation in which she lived was the middle one of the three, and whereby the neighbours at each side of her had their own garden paths which led down to Wide Lane itself, Maud had to go out of her front door, along a pathway that fronted the houses, and use one or other of the exit points.

This all worked out fine until she fell out with both sets of adjacent inhabitants, and she confided in my mam about her concerns. "What if I die, Sally?" she said tearfully. "The neighbours won't let them carry me out down their paths. The undertaker will have to take me round the back, down the field, and lift me over a five-barred gate! I couldn't live with that."

Poor Maud.

The Horror Of It All

When Mam and I were still in our house on Troy Road, the relative of a girl who was in our 'gang' when we were kids, lived a few doors further down the street. The girl was about fourteen while I was ten, and lived with an elderly lady who could have been her mother or grandmother – I'm not quite sure. And she altered clothing at home for people in the neighbourhood.

The two of us were in the house when the lady was busy on her sewing machine when after a while she let out a cry of pain. Both my friend and I ran over to see that the needle had gone straight through a finger-nail, pinning the woman's finger to the base of the machine. She had to turn the wheel with her other hand until the needle was out and then go and dress her wound. It was a sickening experience.

The other involved my aunt Maria. (How did you guess?) We had moved to Newlands by this time, and Aunt Maria was on a visit. Unfortunately, Mam and I had to go out for an hour, and Mam had to explain to my aunt how to use the electric stove since Aunt Maria was only familiar with gas. We didn't have an electric kettle at the time and had to use our old 'whistler' on the new stove until we could afford something better. Anyhow, the use of the hotplates was explained to my aunt, whereby she said, "Aye. I'm not stupid, Sal. I know what to do so you two get off." So we did.

Before we got back, Aunt Maria must have decided to make herself some tea, and while she was waiting for the tea mashing, she took it upon herself to wash down the wall above the cooker with the spare hot water – considering, I guess, that it needed a bit of a clean. So, she got a stool, balanced upon it, and deciding that she wasn't close enough to the wall, knelt on top of the stove. Yes, the hotplate was still on and it fused one of her stockings into the flesh of her knee. She thought that since she couldn't see a flame, it was off.

When we arrived back home, Mam and I had to try and free the stocking from her skin, and clean and bandage her knee. My mother said she ought to go to the doctor – or even hospital – but Aunt Maria wouldn't. In those days, women didn't seem to fuss over anything, but to me, it was another distressing episode.

Eyes Down

My mother was a feisty Yorkshire woman.

When we lived on Hunger Hill, she tackled our next door neighbour because her son – who was older than I – had been bullying me. She went next door to complain, but when the woman just laughed in Mam's face, she dragged her over the doorstep and pummelled her. I was never bullied again. Then when we lived on Newlands Drive, my mother often used to go to afternoon bingo at the Morley Pavilion and I always asked her how she had got on and she'd tell me everything that had transpired.

One day when she came home, I asked again as usual, and she said, "You know her from the Crescent: the one whose sons are allus in and art o' prison?" I had no idea, so asked Mam what she looked like. "She's the one wi' a face like a cow's arse!" says Mam. (I was none the wiser.) "Anyway," she went on, "in the interval yer can bet tanners on cards, and whatever card is drawn out of another pack, you win what's on it. Anyroad, I won all these tanners and she says to me, ''Ere, Sally lass, gi' us a few o' yer winnin's so I can 'ave another go.'"

"And did you?" I asked. "Did I 'ell as like," she said. "I just told 'er that my name were Hunt."

I never quite understood that?

What's In A Name?

My mother had an unusual wont of describing the women she knew by either their appearance or personal preferences in certain areas.

One was 'Shacker' (Shaker) because of the way she'd constantly jingle the bus fare in her glove – which used to drive Mam to distraction before the bus turned up. Another was a tall and upright lady who was known as Stiff Elsie, and then there was one who suffered with flatulence and whose name was alliteratively convenient – she was known as Farting Freda.

Also within Mam's coterie, were many Lilys. There was Lily the Pink and Lily the Black – named so for their liking for men of different races; then there was one whose name I never really understood when I was young, and she, apparently, was overly fond of the male sex. She was known as Dick Lily. And, according to my mother, was: "Very good with her hand."

I'm not surprised I never knew how to address them whenever I was introduced – or if I even dare!

Horse Sense

I always recall the time when my aunt Maria first got a TV and a film of the Queen at trooping the colour came on when programmes were finishing. (There was only one channel in those days.) Every single night, without fail, she'd stare at the screen, saying, "She ought t'be in bed be nar, 'stead o' ridin' round on a bloody 'orse."

On another occasion, I remember a neighbour showing her an album of photographs displaying some of her past relatives. "Now, this one here," said the neighbour pointing at one of the old sepia pictures, "is my grandfather, Hercules."

And Aunt Maria said questioningly, "Bloody Hercules? That's ludicrous. Fancy calling a lad after Steptoe's horse!" My aunt was deliciously droll.

A further example of her unworldly charm was when my mam was telling her of a man she knew on Newlands who worked at a factory where they rendered animal by-products. "He's up to here" – she indicated the top of each arm – "in mucky water."

"Eeh, Sally, that's ridic'lous," said my aunt. "The poor bugger could drown!"

"What?" said Mam. "Nay, Maria. I mean 'is *arms* are in mucky water not 'is whole bloody body!"

Part Three
Goodbye Short Trousers

Mountaineering

I hated Morley Grammar School when I first started there. I had lost the majority of my pals from Peel Street who had gone to other schools and I felt lonely and abandoned.

Because my mother worked – and I didn't have a house key of my own – I often used to run away from school and hide in my aunts' house. Both were annoyed at me, and Aunt Maria was convinced that the bobbies would come and lock her up for harbouring a criminal.

But one day the kid-catcher, 'Pug' Jackson, found out where I was hiding, and came for me. I argued with him, saying I was never going back to the place. Hammer and tongs I went at him before I finally bolted out of the open door, along the landing, and fled across Troy Road. Then I went down the side of the houses which were there at the time, and jumped down a small wall, after which I travelled on to a precipitous area behind the Rock Inn. It was a treacherous venture, but I was like a mountain goat and managed to climb up to an area of trees at the higher side of Troy – and stayed there until I thought it safe to go back to my aunts.

I cannot remember if Pug was still there or not when I finally went back, but over the weeks and months I did settle into grammar school life.

Across The Country

I had a few different PT teachers at Morley Grammar, and each was, in their own nasty way, heartless.

One used to make certain boys hang from the wall-bars, stick his thumb on their sternum and push violently. There was no rhyme or reason for his actions – he was just a sick, sadistic swine. If he would have tried that with me – young though I was – I'd have landed him one.

The other one couldn't wait for the bitterness of winter to strike, and joyfully make us kit out in T-shirts and shorts and go on a cross-country run. We'd be escorted up to Britannia Road, and were then sent out across the fields all the way to Howden Clough and back again – an exhaustingly long way to go in snow and ice.

I remember once how myself and a pal lagged behind the pack, and when we got half-way round the course, hid in a shed that was conveniently situated on the route. We'd stay there, clinging together for warmth, until the other lads could be heard passing on their way back, constantly peering out of the shed to see a convenient break in the flow of bodies so that we could nip in and make our way back as though we'd run all the way.

Back at school, our fingers were so numb we found it difficult to button the shirts of our school uniform. It was then the teacher came into the changing-rooms and pointed at we two miscreants – we had been discovered. How he caught us out for not completing the course I don't know, but he must have had his spies out – or somebody snitched on us.

We were both dispatched to the headmaster – who I found to be a decidedly fair-minded man – and given an hour's detention. The punishment was to go and make sure the books in the library were arranged neatly, and alphabetically, on the shelves; and apart from being late home, it was a joy to do.

After all, the place was nice and warm.

The Neighbour

The back doors of the houses on Newlands Drive were actually at the sides of the semi-detached dwellings.

Our door faced a neighbour's where Betty lived, and she used to chat to my mother over the privet hedge that separated the buildings from each other.

On a bright summer Monday – a day of the week when everybody seemed to do their washing – both women were hanging out the wash on the lines in the back gardens. Having done ours, Mam asked me to wipe out the twin-tub while she finished the pegging out, which I did. But since the back door was open, I could hear her and Betty chatting over the hedge as per usual – both being unaware that I was eavesdropping.

"Sally," Betty said to Mam. "What do you do about yer...yer know?" Naturally, my mother was at a loss as to what our neighbour was talking about, so said, "My what, Betty?"

After a long pause, Betty says, "About yer bloomers?" And Mam said, "Nay, lass. I don't wear damn bloomers! I wear knickers and they're on the line."

"Eeh, I say. But what if your David sees 'em?" Betty asked. "And keep yer voice down, love, in case t'neighbours are list'nin'."

I think by this time, Mam was at a loss as to where the conversation was heading as she said, "What does it matter if he does?"

"Nay, lass," said Betty; "yer can't be letting young lads see stuff like that. My Joe (her son) is much too young to be sullied by t'sight o' me unmentionables 'angin' art in case he comes visitin'."

"Oh for God's sake, Betty," my mother answered. "Your Joe's thirty-six and he's got three kids."

And I returned to wiping out the washer – not without a smile on my face.

Gravity Took Over

My mother and I had done some shopping in Morley for my aunt.

Whilst walking down Zoar Street on the way to Troy Road, laden with a couple of bags each, I suddenly sensed that my mum was lagging behind, and in turning back, saw her standing in the middle of the street with her knickers round her ankles. The elastic had gone. Well, I could do little but laugh while she stood there in shock. "Get back here," were her words uttered in whispers in case somebody heard. So I did.

Taking the bags from her, she had to step out of the said garment as she looked about her to see if anyone was watching. "I'll be the talk of the bloody town," she cursed, throwing the knickers in one of the bags. "And all you can do is laugh!"

When we reached my aunt's house, Mam emptied the shopping – including the discarded garment – when they were spotted by Aunt Maria. "What the 'ell are *them*?" she asked.

"Mam's knickers," said I.

My aunt was indignant. "Good Lord, Sally," she said. "Surely y'aven't been gettin' up to tricks? Not in broad daylight!"

Mam's simple response was: "Oh, shut up – both of yer."

By The Book

When we are young – or even still these days – we usually consider our mothers as being virginal, unsullied and, in a way, sexless. Often we think that, maybe, we were indeed found under a gooseberry bush, unable to contemplate what our parents actually did to bring us into this world. Then suddenly, something transpires to completely dispel our misguided beliefs; and this happened to me at the age of fifteen.

You'll have gathered by now that our house on Newlands Drive was all electric. Apart from the cooker, we had been provided with a large container to use for boiling any white items that needed a wash; and one day when Mam had gone to afternoon bingo, I thought I'd help out by doing the bedding – and other suitable things which were stored in said boiler. So I sorted out the whites from the coloured ones; and then to my astonishment, concealed beneath the lot, was a copy of a book. In that enlightening moment, I recognised that my mother was a woman in all senses of the word; and needless to say, the washing never got done.

By the way, the book was Lady Chatterley's Lover.

Just The Tonic

When Mam had managed to buy me a bicycle to travel to Morley Grammar School and I obtained a dynamo to provide lighting for my bike, I often visited Aunt Maria in the dark nights of winter. So on one of those wintry nights, I went to see her, and she welcomed me with open arms. And as per usual, she was sitting in front of the fire as I entered the house. I knew my cousin would have gone to the working men's club, so I sat down, whence my aunt said, "Eeh, lad; yer look frozzen to de'ath....I know! I've got just the stuff to cure that." And she got up and went to the scullery where I heard her rooting about for something or other.

On her return, she said, "'Ere, get that darn yer. It'll warm yer up. But don't tell yer mam or our Tony or there'll be 'ell ter pay." So I put the glass of liquid to my lips and drank – and coughed. "Good, init?" says she, and I nodded. "'Er next door" – she pointed at the wall – "made it. It's bilb'rry wine and'll keep out t'cold. She goes down t'Station Road bankin' to collect 'em, so sup up, lad, an' then yer can 'ave another." So I did.

How I cycled home I'll never know. But before I left, my devout and staid Aunt Maria said, "I'd best not 'ave any more, or when our Tony comes in 'e'll think I'm" – she hiccuped – "pissed."

Flightless

Now, admit it, we do tend to laugh instead of feeling sympathy for someone who falls in an odd way, and it happened to me when I was a sixteen-year-old – and it involved my mother.

Having done some shopping in Morley, we were walking down Peel Street and along Albert Road to our home on Newlands Drive.

Eventually, we reached a point where Albert Road veers right on its way to Wide Lane, and on the corner was a patch of grass which we had to go over before reaching the road itself.

Unfortunately, my mother tripped at the start of the grassy area, but didn't fall immediately: she kept on going like an ostrich, before dropping at the far end of the grass still hanging on to the shopping with arms and legs splayed. I just remained on the pavement and laughed my socks off, before putting down my own bags and going to help her up. The only hurt she suffered was embarrassment, but once dusted down, she slapped me on the arm, saying, "That was all your bloody fault!"

Why me? Again?

Missing Him

I barely remember my father, but Mam did say that I had his head for figures – yet was also possessed of her own spirited temperament. But then there came a day in my presence when her resolve failed her....

Shortly before my nineteenth birthday, the gossip of neighbours reached Mam's ears. And observing me bring quite a few young men home – some highly more camp than I have ever been – she confronted me.

"David. I want you to be truthful with me."

I was quiet. I knew she had twigged about my burgeoning homosexuality. I say 'burgeoning', but I had known from an early age that I was different from most other lads.

Noticing my silent reticence, she spoke further: "Folk are saying you're – oh! how I hate this word – queer. Well?"

After the longest of moments, I said quietly, "They call it gay these days."

"Do they…? Well, you don't look too bloody happy to *me*."

"But I am Mam, Honestly, I am!"

She surprised me then by saying, "Right! Then so am I. And if yer dad were here, so would he be. He'd 'ave loved yer even if yer 'ad two 'eads, and both faces were like slapped arses." She smiled…but then her eyes filled with tears and I rushed to her and held her. "I still miss him, David," she sobbed. "Even now, after all these years, I still miss yer dad."

As I held her in my arms, she wept. And when she couldn't cry any more, she stroked my hand that was resting on her shoulder, saying, "Aay, lad. I hope yer find some'dy one day as good as yer dad were. And I hope he stays with yer for a long, long time." She pulled away from me now, and placed both hands on my face. And as she smiled once more, she said, "By God! yer do look like him."

Where There's Muck

You will have learned by now that I spent a lot of time at my aunt Maria's, and also know of the trouble she had with words and phrases – often coming out with unintended spoonerisms. Well here is an example of the use of a word that she didn't understand in the context in which it was said....

One day while we were at my aunt's house on Troy Road, my mam was engaged in reading the local newspaper. Suddenly she said, "Well, well. Just listen to this, Maria! Ernie Sedgewick has died on his own premises and left a fortune."

"Eeh," said my aunt, "just goes to show. D'yer know, he never 'ad a brass farthin' when he were a lad. He used to go around wi' cardboard in 'is shoes to block up t''oiles."

"Well, apparently," says Mam, "he made a pile in the mill."

None the wiser, Aunt Maria said in her usual ingenuous manner: "Poor bugger. Mind you, I'm not surprised 'cos he allus 'ad loose bowels."

The look on my mother's face was priceless.

When I'm Gone

Peter and I started our forty-two year relationship as pen-pals, and were fortunate to find each other via the Melody Maker music magazine of the 1960s. He lived in Manchester, and for four years we travelled back and forth over the Pennines on alternate weekends. When he first came to Morley, my mam took to him immediately, and they both grew to love each other like a mother would for a new son. And there was another bonus for her: he had trained – and worked – as a hairdresser.

One day at the end of October, Mam decided to get the Christmas cake mixed and baked. She had already soaked the fruit in rum for a week, and getting it out of the pantry, said, "'Ere, you two, come an' smell this." And she stuck the bowl under our noses. "It fair makes yer 'air curl. And talkin' about 'air, just look at it! And I'm goin' to bingo t'neet. It could do wi' colourin'."

"Well," Pete said, "if you have the dye, I'll do it for you."

"Will yer, lad?" Mam says. "Eeh, that'll be grand. There's some in one of the drawers. Mind you, I'll 'ave to carry on wi' t'cake 'cos I've started it nar." And so the hair dyeing and cake mixing ran in tandem.

"I got 'Autumn Glow'," Mam said, "Whatever the 'ell that is? I 'ope it'll be all reight."

"It'll suit you, Mrs Morris," (he always called her that) and then started the job over the kitchen sink. But seeing the dye being rinsed off, my mam caught sight of the colour. "Nay, it's bloody mauve!" But Peter reassured her it would be fine.

"Oh, damn," says Mam abruptly. "The cake!" And she immediately turned from the sink to the baking-bowl where, sure enough, as she stirred the heavy mixture, the dye dripped into the Christmas cake. "Bugger it," said she. "Well, it'll 'ave to stay in now. I'm not startin' it all over again."

With her hair done and styled, she got to bingo to have the look admired by all and sundry. And when Christmas arrived and the three of us were together enjoying a slice of cake with a piece of Wensleydale cheese, Mam had to admit that it was the best cake she'd ever made.

Later, when we were partaking of a few drinks, she suddenly said to Peter, "You love our David, don't yer, lad?" I was stunned!

And Pete, after a long pause, said, "Yes. Yes I do, Mrs Morris."

"Good! Then when I'm gone, make sure yer keep him safe 'cos he can be a reight bugger at times. And for God's sake, stop calling me Mrs Morris."

Now, she leaned back in her chair, took a sip of her cream sherry, and smiled.

The End
or as we say in Yorkshire:
T'End

Printed in Great Britain
by Amazon